AMERICAN REFUGEES

A portion of the proceeds from sales of American Refugees *will be donated to*

Shooting Back, an education and media resource center for homeless children,

1901 18th Street, NW, Washington, DC 20009.

AMERICAN REFUGEES

JIM HUBBARD

Foreword by Jonathan Kozol

University of Minnesota Press
Minneapolis Oxford

Published by the University of Minnesota Press
2037 University Avenue Southeast, Minneapolis, MN 55414
Printed in the United States of America

The University of Minnesota Press gratefully
acknowledges typesetting assistance provided for this
book by Northwestern Printcrafters, Inc.

Photo editor: Mike Zerby

Design and layout: Sheila Chin Morris

Library of Congress Cataloging-in-Publication Data
Hubbard, Jim, 1942-
    American refugees/Jim Hubbard; foreword by Jonathan Kozol.
        p. cm.
    ISBN 0-8166-1896-8 ISBN 0-8166-1927-1 (pbk.)
    1. Homeless persons—United States—Pictorial works. I. Title.
HV4505.H83 1991   90-49448
362.5'0973—dc20   CIP
A CIP catalog record for this book is available from the British Library

The University of Minnesota is an equal-opportunity educator and employer

DEDICATION

To Sherry,

Priya and Hanna,

and in the memory of

Brijin Marie

FOREWORD   The widening gulf between the rich and the poor in the United States finds no manifestation quite so bitter as the sight of homeless people, particularly families, wandering the streets and finding respite in the subways, alleys, and shelters of our major cities. My first introduction to these modern American exiles was in the largest family shelter of New York—a huge and squalid building, once a luxury hotel, situated just a few steps from Fifth Avenue. In this building, which reminded me of nothing else so much as an internment camp for urban refugees, some sixteen hundred people—two-thirds of them children—lived in conditions that I'd never seen before outside of the Third World. ★ The year was 1985. The conscience of the nation, although increasingly hardened by the values of the Reagan age, did not yet seem utterly resistant to the contemplation of injustice, nor to indignation and compassion. Press reports, though seasonal and sporadic, tended nonetheless to focus on the human anguish of the victims, and not on the inconvenience to the well-to-do who were compelled to view them on their way to offices in nearby modern high-rise buildings. ★ Today the nation's mood has changed from sadness to impatience. Far from feeling troubled or guilt-ridden, New York City's influential citizens—particularly the editors and writers of the city's daily press—seem to feel angry that the numbers of the poor and homeless have continued to increase, as if they somehow had invested something of themselves in feeling "sad" and "generous" for three or four brief years and now must overcome their instincts of compassion if they are to carry on their ordinary lives with the required feelings of immunity to suffering. ★ In Washington, Chicago, San Francisco, and many other cities, much the same trend is evident. Press reports speak of the inconvenience to affluent commuters who are forced to look into the eyes of homeless people at close hand or even asked to reach into their pockets for a dollar or a dime that will no doubt, as press reports suggest, be used for drugs or a bottle of cheap wine. New York City now congratulates itself, as Nazi Germany might once have done, upon its toughness in removing "undesirables" from public places. An influential columnist, George Will, subsumes the ethos of the age by telling us to view this as a "hygiene" problem rather than an ethical concern. The attitude is: "Get them out of sight, where I don't have to see them." While cuts in housing funds and health services continue unabated, our cities and states are busily constructing bigger prisons. ★ The power of Jim Hubbard's photographs forces us to confront the human price that has been paid for these unspeakable injustices. They are not simply stunning photographs; they are also life-affirming. For they show us that there is a certain capability for love and hope and joy that even society's most ruthless, unforgivable dismissal has not been able to destroy. ★ But I believe it is the faces of the children here that will stir the strongest and most visceral response. A little girl stares into the lens, her hair disheveled, in her tiny arms a doll. She looks at us with eyes that no one whose humanity has not been totally congealed can meet without a sense of shame and fear. She and the other children in this book tell us of the crime of a rich nation that can celebrate its Wall Street traders and its corporate executives while shunning those who, for no reason but the accidents of birth and circumstance, are left to wander in a darkness that will someday cast its shadow on us all. Open these pages with great caution. What you see will not make sleeping easy. The children you will see will haunt your deepest dreams. Their eyes will ask you questions that have not been answered. JONATHAN KOZOL

PREFACE   When I was a boy, growing up in Detroit, my father used to take me to see the so-called derelicts

who lived on the streets of the skid row areas. He wanted me to learn a lesson by observation, and I was indeed

intensely curious about the people I saw there: I wanted to know who they were, where they had come from,

and what happened to them. I carried this curiosity with me into adulthood when I worked as a photographer

for the *Detroit News*. While there I covered the 1967 riots, and it was through them that I was introduced to

issues of poverty, racism, and disenfranchisement. I was also at Wounded Knee in 1973 and was disturbed and

saddened by the environment Native Americans and their children had to live in. My realization that the dominant

culture had forcibly hidden these people away played a key role in my decision to use my talents on behalf of the

dispossessed. ★ It was Mitch Snyder who helped me to see the need to live out the ideas I had been struggling

with for many years. Mitch did not simply pay lip service to the gospel message to serve, he accepted it as a

personal call to action. I appreciate the example he offered in shedding indifference and working to help and

protect "the least among us." ★ As you look at these photographs, I urge you to see the similarities between

you and the people shown here. These people are our neighbors. They are like you and me: they've gone to

college, had jobs, and been laid off; they've had families, belonged to churches, and served in the military. But unlike many of us, homeless people have suffered job losses and uninsured illnesses they could not prevent; many of them are the deinstitutionalized mentally ill, released into a society they can neither comprehend nor defend themselves against. It is often overlooked that many homeless people work, but they lack the "safety nets" (savings accounts, supportive relatives, friends who can lend money) that many of us take for granted. Housing costs have risen far beyond what their low incomes can accommodate, and the government they support by paying taxes, just as you and I do, has abdicated its responsibility to ensure that they have decent, affordable housing. In this sense homeless people are indeed American refugees. Not only have they been forced into exile by catastrophic circumstances that are beyond their control, but their separation from the predominant culture is as total as if they had been deported to another land. ★ The images included here are slices of the lives of impoverished human beings, but I hope they offer a perspective that other photographic treatments of homelessness do not have. As a photographer, I have shared the lives of homeless people for ten years, and I consider it a blessing to have had my life enriched by this involvement. It is my hope that I have captured the humanity, the vitality, the dignity, and the importance of the people represented here. My work has also been motivated by my desire to affect what I consider a blaming, intolerant, and unjust society in which not only individuals, but mothers, fathers, and children—whole families—are being put aside and discounted. Today, hundreds of thousands of children are growing up in shelters, on the streets, and even in cars, abandoned by a system that should be caring for and nurturing them. I offer my photographs as evidence of this unacceptable reality. I hope through them to move others to share in the struggles and despair of homeless people and to work together to make our system more humane and more accountable. ★ Proverbs tells us that whoever has pity on the poor lends to the Lord and will be repaid. I know this to be true in my own life, and I believe that nothing takes precedence over this mandate. I also believe that how we meet this challenge will determine the essence of our society for decades to come. JIM HUBBARD

ACKNOWLEDGMENTS

Many individuals and organizations have contributed toward the fulfillment of this project. I extend my gratitude for their generous gifts of time, encouragement, and support:

Herb & Lou Benson
Beth & Margo
Amy Bowerman
Philip Brookman
Michael Burton
Peter Carlson
Stephanie Clohesy
Terry Cochran
Tony Coelho
Anne Edelstein
Suzy Farren
Carol Fennelly
Angela Fitzgerald & Family
Betsy Frampton
Claude Francke
Thelma Goettling
Pat Hanrahan
Dana Harris
Mary Ellen Hombs
Frank Howard
Peter Howe
Lois Hubbard
Kathy & Katrina Hurt
Donald Irish
Vanessa Johnson & Family
Laura Kuff
Sue & Mitchell Kuff
Sharon Ladin
Lynn Lester
Dr. Douglas Lewis
Elliot Liebow
Joy Lovinger
Ella McCall

Rueben McCornack
Patti Mercure
Lisa Mihaly
Barbara & Jesse Mishler
Sheila Chin Morris
Lindsey Plexico
Julio Quan
Larry Rasmussen
Nancy Sanford
Martin Sheen
Robin Smith
Jane Southwood
Michael Stoops
Fred Sweets
Mike Zerby

At the University of Minnesota Press:
   Mary Byers
   Craig Carnahan
   Lisa Freeman
   Pat Gonzales
   Susan Marsnik
   Susan Wakefield
   Kathy Wolter

American Institute of Architects
Asman Lab
Cafritz Foundation
Carpenter Shelter
Catholic Health Association
Childrens Defense Fund
Chrome, Inc.
College of St. Thomas

Communications Consortium
Community for Creative Non-Violence
Community Foundation
Community of Hope
Enterprise Foundation
Exodus Youth Services
Garrett Lab
Glen Eagles
Hamline University
Homeless Information Exchange
House of Ruth
Ilford
Image, Inc.
Kellogg National Fellowship Program
Life Magazine
Meyer Foundation
Mitchell & Company
National Association of Social Workers
National Coalition for the Homeless
Pro Photo
Public Welfare Foundation
Reston Shelter
Urban Institute
League of Women Voters
Video Action Fund
The Washington Post
Washington Project for the Arts
Wesley Theological Seminary
World Vision

AMERICAN REFUGEES

An American woman

THE FITZGERALD FAMILY

In August of 1987, Angela Fitzgerald and her four children were served an eviction notice from their home in

Dominion Gardens, a low-income housing project located in the affluent Washington, D.C., suburb of Alexandria,

Virginia. A single parent, Angela was at the time of her eviction employed by the Social Security Administration.

Following news of her impending eviction, Angela and her neighbors organized a demonstration to protest the decision to close Dominion Gardens. The complex had been slated for renovation into middle-income dwellings whose rents current tenants would not have been able to afford. Angela had fallen behind in her payments before the closing of the project.

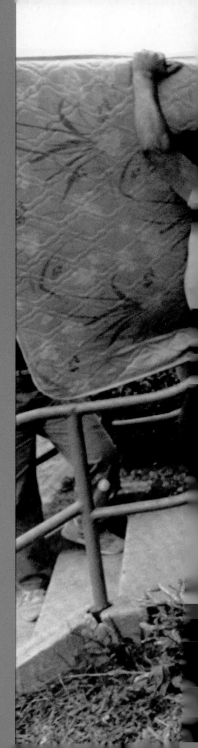

4 An American man

6 An American child

PUBLIC REFUGEES

In the early 1980s, the Reagan administration assured Americans that there were no homeless in America. When I began photographing the homeless in 1980, I first saw those whose lives are lived in public spaces, the visible, yet invisible, the homeless people whom we have come to call "bag ladies," "derelicts," and "bums." ★ For those who exist in public view, there is no privacy. Loneliness and isolation define their days, and the only sense of permanence comes from the certainty that they will eventually be told to move on.

10

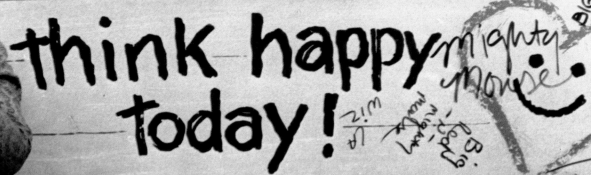

REFUGEE CHILDREN

As I continued my work among the homeless, I realized that my initial photographs

had only scratched the surface of the problem. Behind the public scenes are those

less obvious. Many of the homeless are unwilling victims too young to have any

choice. It is estimated that one-quarter of the homeless in America are children,

and the homeless population is increasingly made up of families.

Cornell Hatton pauses near an abandoned building owned and managed by the Department of Housing Preservation and Development of the City of New York.

Annette Wilson walks through her neighborhood in the South Bronx, a landscape reminiscent of foreign war zones.

George Cook stares in quiet anger as his family is evicted from
their home.

For many homeless children, games have given way to grim
reality. This young man is proud of his starter pistol.

Fear is reflected in Andrea Jones's face as she watches her
bedroom furniture being moved onto the sidewalk during another
eviction.

Mary Fitzgerald waits for the Sheriff's Department to arrive to evict her family.

Cornell Hatton "at home."

A young girl in rural Mississippi. Her home is a rough shack.

Shut in and shut out, these children play behind the Capitol City   33
Inn, a motel used to house the homeless during the 1980s. At
least five children are known to have died there in recent years.
The Capitol City Inn is now closed.

Mary (10) and Michelle (8 months) were not at the time fully aware of what was   39

happening to them.

40   The process of eviction is both dehumanizing and total. Little is left to choice or chance.

In addition to furniture and personal belongings, the Fitzgeralds' pets were also evicted. Unlike the Fitzgeralds themselves, however, their cats were taken to a shelter.

44   Once evicted, the family was left to fend for themselves.

Ultimately, Angela found space for herself and her three youngest children in

Christ House, a homeless shelter in Old Town Alexandria; their new neighbors

showed little interest in their plight.

Mary (10) and Amanda (6) gradually came to resist the idea of being photographed. Left without a home and having been denied the rights of due process on several counts, their only means of escape was play.

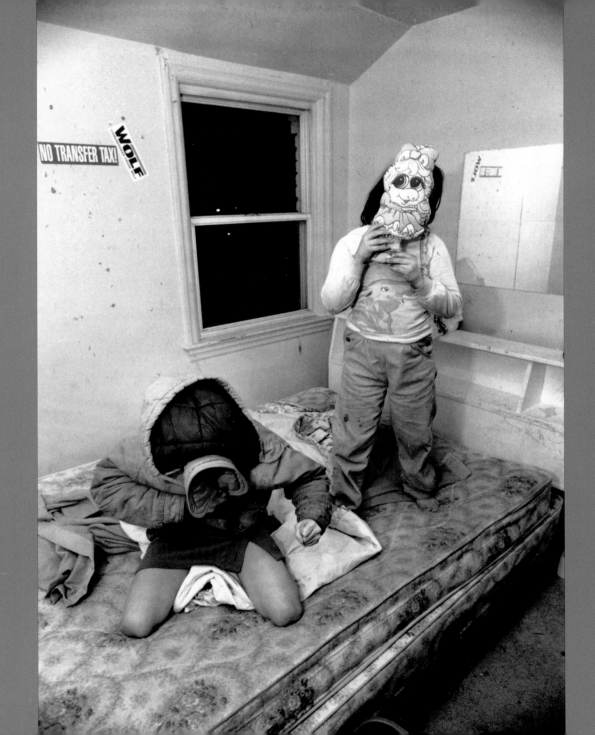

49

From the shelter, the Fitzgeralds moved into smaller quarters in Section 8 housing. Dennis Fitzgerald (13) was, through the efforts of a determined attorney, enrolled in a school for gifted children when it was discovered that his IQ approached the genius range. Angela Fitzgerald and her three youngest children moved to Virginia Beach shortly after this photograph was taken.

For the homeless, the normal events of everyday life are more often attempts—

sometimes successful, sometimes not—at making do, getting by, hanging on.

Even in shelters, which are frequently overcrowded, everyday life is little better

than life on the streets. For some, even shelter life is not an option.

As in most shelters, life at the Capitol City Inn (*left*), a motel formerly used to house homeless families, and at the Community for Creative Non-Violence shelter (*right*), is regulated by a series of rules.

The Carpenter Shelter in Alexandria, Virginia, is a converted warehouse.

In the women's section, a thin curtain across the cubicle entrance
provides a vague semblance of privacy.

Many of the cubicles are "home" to families and children.

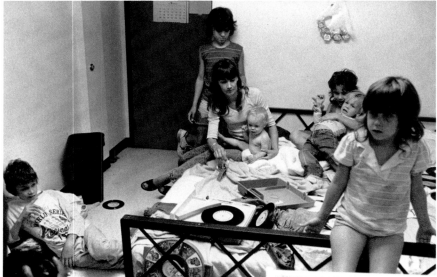

60   Common spaces at the Carpenter Shelter *(upper left and upper right)* provide some opportunity for children to play, but for the adults, a single television provides the only distraction from the

daily monotony. At other shelters—in the wealthy suburb of
Reston, Virginia *(lower left)*, and at the Capitol City Inn (now
closed)—large families often live in single rooms.

62   Quiet times together are often possible only in impersonal surroundings.

For other families, a shelter is not an option. Joshua, Rachel, and their four children lived in the cab of their pickup truck for six months.

Christopher and Harriet Moore and their four children live in their van in a park, because they cannot afford housing in the affluent northern Virginia suburbs. Christopher is a laid-off systems analyst.

Still other families have been forced to live in campgrounds.

68

For many homeless families, clothing is available only through charities, which deliver truckloads of castoffs. Finding wearable clothes in appropriate sizes is another matter, however.

70   Obtaining food is often a tiring and demeaning process, even in the nation's capital on Christmas Eve.

Food lines are often long and inclement weather is little deterrence. For young and old alike, food supplied by charitable organizations is often the only nourishment available.

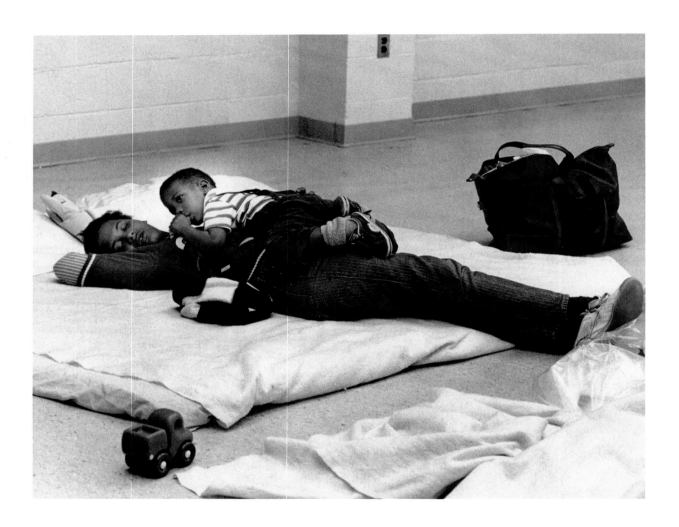

Undisturbed sleep is an unknown luxury in most shelters.

Several men shared this bed near the Watergate Hotel.

In the midst of a blizzard, a subway grate provides a trace of warmth for sleeping; although not on the usual tour of Washington's monuments, it is a sight that tourists gawk at.

80   The following list of statewide homeless, housing, and rural housing coalitions and state government contacts was prepared by the National Coalition for the Homeless. For further information, please contact the Coalition, 1621 Connecticut Avenue, Washington, DC 20009, (202) 265-2371.

ALABAMA

Alabama Department of Economic and Community Affairs
Community Services Division
Joe McNees/Andre Epps
3465 Norman Bridge Road
Montgomery, AL 36105
   Phone: 205-284-8955
   Fax: 205-284-8670

Alabama Low Income Housing Coalition
Cleo Askew
P.O. Box 95
Epes, AL 35460
   Phone: 205-652-9676

ALASKA

Alaska Coalition for the Homeless
Paul Day
c/o Department of Community and Regional Affairs
949 East 36th Street, Suite 402
Anchorage, AK 99508
   Phone: 907-563-1073

Department of Community and Regional Affairs
State of Alaska
David G. Hoffman
P.O. Box B
Juneau, AK 99801
   Phone: 907-465-4700
   Fax: 907-465-2948

ARIZONA

Arizona Department of Economic Security
Community Services Administration
Karen Novachek
P.O. Box 6123 Site Code 0867
Phoenix, AZ 85005
   Phone: 602-229-2736
   Fax: 602-229-2782

Homeless Task Force/Arizona Human Services Coalition
W. Mark Clark
c/o Traveler's Aid
40 West Veterans Boulevard
Tucson, AZ 85713
   Phone: 602-622-8900
   Fax: 602-622-2964

ARKANSAS

Alliance of Shelter Providers
Joe Flaherty
c/o Our House
P.O. Box 34155
Little Rock, AR 72203
   Phone: 501-375-2416

Office of Community Services
Thomas Green
P.O. Box 1437/Slot 1330
Little Rock, AR 72203
   Phone: 501-682-8715
   Fax: 501-682-6571

CALIFORNIA

California Coalition for Rural Housing (CCRH)
Callie Hutchison
2000 "O" Street, Suite 230
Sacramento, CA 95814
   Phone: 916-443-5128
   Fax: 916-442-7966
   Handsnet: HN0006

California Homeless Coalition
Kay Knepprath
926 "J" Street, Suite 906
Sacramento, CA 95814
   Phone: 916-447-0390
   Handsnet: HN0046

California Homeless Coalition
Toni Reinis
1010 South Flower Street, Suite 500
Los Angeles, CA 90015
   Phone: 213-746-7690
   Fax: 213-748-2432
   Handsnet: HN0047

California Right to Housing Campaign
Marc Brown
2000 "O" Street, Suite 230
Sacramento, CA 95814
   Phone: 916-443-5128

Orange County Housing Now Coalition
Tim Carpenter
1440 E. 1st Street, Room 406
Santa Ana, CA 92701
   Phone: 714-835-8718

Health and Welfare Agency/Office of the Secretary
Margaret Debow
1600 Ninth Street, Suite 450
Sacramento, CA 95814
    Phone: 916-445-0196
    Fax: 916-445-1549

COLORADO

Colorado Affordable Housing Partnership
Barry Booker
1981 Blake Street
Denver, CO 80202
    Phone: 303-297-2548
    Fax: 303-297-2615

Colorado Coalition for the Homeless
John Parvensky/Mary Wilham
2100 Broadway
Denver, CO 80205
    Phone: 303-293-2217

Colorado Division of Housing
John Maldonado
1313 Sherman, Suite 323
Denver, CO 80203
    Phone: 303-866-2033
    Fax: 303-866-4465

Governor's Task Force on the Homeless
Swanee Hunt
1981 Blake Street
Denver, CO 80202
    Phone: 303-297-7355

CONNECTICUT

Connecticut Coalition for the Homeless
Jane McNichol
30 Jordan Lane
Wethersfield, CT 06109
    Phone: 203-721-7876

Connecticut Housing Coalition
Jeff Freiser
30 Jordan Lane
Wethersfield, CT 06109
    Phone: 203-563-2943

Department of Human Resources
Elliot Ginsberg/Alan Carbenneau
1049 Asylum Avenue
Hartford, CT 06105
    Phone: 203-566-3318
    Fax: 203-566-7613

DELAWARE

Delaware Coalition for the Homeless/
Delaware Housing NOW
Ken Smith-Shuman
P.O. Box 25291
Wilmington, DE 19899
    Phone: 302-656-1667 or 302-762-2779
    Handsnet: HN1110

Delaware Housing Coalition
Dolores Solberg
317 Treadway Tower
9 East Loockerman Street
Dover, DE 19901
    Phone: 302-678-2286
    Handsnet: HN0769

Division of Community Services
Department of Community Affairs
Dennis Savage/Frances West
820 North French Street, 4th floor
Wilmington, DE 19801
    Phone: 302-577-3491
    Fax: 302-577-2621

DISTRICT OF COLUMBIA

Churches Conference on Shelter and Housing
Keary Kincannon
1711 14th Street, NW
Washington, DC 20009
    Phone: 202-232-6748

Department of Human Services
Janice Woodward
801 N. Capital Street, NE, Suite 700
Washington, DC 20002
    Phone: 202-724-8815
    Fax: 202-724-4346

Community for Creative Non-Violence/Housing Now
Carol Fennelly
425 2nd Street, NW
Washington, DC 20001
    Phone: 202-393-1909 or 202-393-4409

DC Commission on Homelessness
Annie Goodson
801 North Capitol Street, NE, Suite 700
Washington, DC 20002
    Phone: 202-727-0518

Mayor's Homeless Coordinating Council
Ken Long
609 "H" Street, NE, 5th floor
Washington, DC 20002
    Phone: 202-727-5930

The Community Partnership for the Prevention
   of Homelessness
Sue Marshall/Linda Davis
1700 Pennsylvania Avenue, NW, Suite 800
Washington, DC 20006
   Phone: 202-624-7525
   Fax: 202-737-0410 or 202-737-2345

Women's Shelter Providers
Tracy Newell
c/o New Endeavors for Women
611 "N" Street, NW
Washington, DC 20001
   Phone: 202-682-5825

FLORIDA

Florida Coalition for the Homeless
Fred Karnas, Jr.
P.O. Box 76301
Tampa, FL 33675
   Phone: 407-425-5307

Florida Department of HRS
Office of Program Policy and Development
Bill Hanson
1317 Winewood Boulevard
Tallahassee, FL 32399
   Phone: 904-488-2761
   Fax: 904-488-4227

Florida Low Income Housing Coalition
Claudia Frese
P.O. Box 932
Tallahassee, FL 32302
   Phone: 904-878-4219
   Fax: 904-942-6312
   Handsnet: HN0302

Florida Non-Profit Housing
Carol Noel
P.O. Box 1987
Sebring, FL 33871
   Phone: 813-385-2519

Governor's Task Force on Homelessness
Florida Department of HRS
Jill Sander
1317 Winewood Boulevard, Building No. 1, Room 216
Tallahassee, FL 32399
   Phone: 904-488-2761

GEORGIA

Georgia Homeless Resource Network
Bill Holland
363 Georgia Avenue, SE
Atlanta, GA 30312
   Phone: 404-589-9495
   Fax: 404-589-8251

Georgia Housing Coalition
Verlee Fowler
250 Georgia Avenue, SE, Suite 363
Atlanta, GA 30312
   Phone: 404-523-0896

Office of Community and Intergovernmental Resources
Georgia Department of Human Resources
Don Mathis
47 Trinity Avenue, Suite 541-H
Atlanta, GA 30334
   Phone: 404-656-3479
   Fax: 404-651-6884

Special Housing Projects
Georgia Residential Finance Authority
Terry E. Ball
60 Executive Parkway, South, Suite 250
Atlanta, GA 30329
   Phone: 404-320-4840
   Fax: 404-320-4837

HAWAII

Affordable Housing Alliance
Betty Lou Larsen
1164 Bishop Street, Suite 1605
Honolulu, HI 96813
   Phone: 808-536-9758

Hawaii Housing Authority
Aric Arakaki
P.O. Box 17907
Honolulu, HI 96817
   Phone: 808-848-3228
   Fax: 808-848-3313

Homeless Aloha, Inc.
Clarence Liu
333 Queen Street, Suite 408
Honolulu, HI 96813
   Phone: 808-537-1399
   Fax: 808-528-0065

IDAHO

Division of Community Rehabilitation
Department of Health and Welfare
Joseph Brunson
450 West State Street
Boise, ID 83702
   Phone: 208-334-5531

Idaho Migrant Council
Tim Lopez
P.O. Box 490
Caldwell, ID 83606
    Phone: 208-454-1652
    Fax: 208-459-0448

ILLINOIS

Illinois Coalition for the Homeless
Michael Marubio
522 East Monroe Street, Suite 304
Springfield, IL 62705
    Phone: 217-788-8060

Illinois Coalition for the Homeless
Michael Marubio
P.O. Box 2751
Chicago, IL 60690
    Phone: 312-435-4548
    Fax: 312-435-5176
    Handsnet: HN0136

Illinois Department of Public Aid
Kathleen Kustra
Harris Building; 100 South Grand
Springfield, IL 62762
    Phone: 217-782-1200
    Fax: 217-524-5995

Office of the Governor/Human Services
Ginger Ostro
100 West Randolph Street; 16th floor
Chicago, IL 60601
    Phone: 312-814-6725
    Fax: 312-814-5512

Statewide Housing Action Coalition (SHAC)
Fran Tobin
202 South State Street, Suite 1414
Chicago, IL 60604
 Phone: 312-939-6074

INDIANA

Indiana Coalition for the Homeless
Barbara Anderson
c/o Hoosier Valley Economic Opportunity Corporation
P.O. Box 843
Jeffersonville, IN 47130
 Phone: 812-288-6451

Indiana Housing Network
Jim Taylor
c/o Indiana Interreligious Commission on Human Equality
1100 West 42nd Street, Suite 320
Indianapolis, IN 46208
 Phone: 317-924-4226 or 317-924-4245

Office of the Governor
John Delap
Statehouse, Suite 206
Indianapolis, IN 46207
 Phone: 317-232-1079
 Fax: 317-232-3443

IOWA

Department of Economic Development
Lane Palmer
200 East Grand Avenue
Des Moines, IA 50309
 Phone: 515-281-7240
 Fax: 515-281-7276

Iowa Coalition for the Homeless
Ben Zachrich
1111 9th Street, Suite 370
Des Moines, IA 50314
 Phone: 515-244-9748

KANSAS

Kansas Department of Commerce/Office of Housing
Phil Dubach
400 West 8th Street, 5th floor
Topeka, KS 66603
 Phone: 913-296-4100
 Fax: 913-296-5055

Kansas Homeless and Hunger Action Coalition
Jim Olson
c/o CRC; 121 East 6th Street, Suite 4
Topeka, KS 66603
 Phone: 913-233-1365

Topeka Housing and Credit Counseling, Inc.
Karen Hiller
1195 SW Buchanan, Suite 203
Topeka, KS 66604
 Phone: 913-234-0217

KENTUCKY

Advisory Council for the Homeless
Office of the Governor
Joan Taylor
State Capitol
Frankfort, KY 40601
 Phone: 502-564-2735

Cabinet for Human Resources/Office of the Secretary
Pat Wasson
275 East Main Street
Frankfort, KY 40621
    Phone: 502-564-7130
    Fax: 502-564-6546

Federation of Appalachian Housing Enterprises
David Lollis
P.O. Drawer B
Berea, KY 40403
    Phone: 606-986-2321

Kentucky Coalition for the Homeless
Mary Beth Gregg
c/o Welcome House
141 Pike Street
Covington, KY 41011
    Phone: 606-431-8717
    Handsnet: HN0776

LOUISIANA

Division of Community Services Grants Management
Marilyn N. Hayes
P.O. Box 44367
Baton Rouge, LA 70804
    Phone: 504-342-2297
    Fax: 504-342-2268

MAINE

Department of Economic and Community Development
Margaret R. Marshall
State House, Station Suite 130
Augusta, ME 04333
    Phone: 207-289-6800
    Fax: 207-289-2861

Maine Coalition for the Homeless
c/o York County Shelter, Inc.
Donald Gean
P.O. Box 20
Alfred, ME 04002
    Phone: 207-324-1137

MARYLAND

Action for the Homeless
Norma Pinette
2539 St. Paul Street
Baltimore, MD 21218
    Phone: 301-467-3800
    Fax: 301-243-9460
    Handsnet: HN0089

Governor's Advisory Board on Homelessness
Susan Seling
c/o Department of Human Resources
311 West Saratoga Street, Suite 229
Baltimore, MD 21201
    Phone: 301-333-0276

Homeless Services Program
Harriet Goldman
311 West Saratoga Street, Suite 229
Baltimore, MD 21201
    Phone: 301-333-0147
    Fax: 301-333-0392

Maryland Low Income Housing Coalition
Ruth Crystal
28 East Ostend
Baltimore, MD 21230
    Phone: 301-727-4200
    Fax: 301-539-2087

MASSACHUSETTS

Executive Office of Human Services
Division of Homelessness and Housing; Social Policy Unit
Irene Lee
1 Ashburton Place, Suite 1109
Boston, MA 02108
    Phone: 617-727-8036
    Fax: 617-727-1396

Massachusetts Affordable Housing Alliance
Lou Finfer
25 West Street, 3rd floor
Boston, MA 02111
    Phone: 617-728-9100

Massachusetts Coalition for the Homeless
Sue Marsh
33 Farnsworth Street
Boston, MA 02210
    Phone: 617-451-0707
    Handsnet: HN0151

Massachusetts Housing Now
Jim Stewart
c/o First Church Shelter
11 Garden Street
Cambridge, MA 02138
    Phone: 617-661-1873

Massachusetts Shelter Providers Association
Anne Maley
7 Marshall Street
Boston, MA 02118
    Phone: 617-742-3720
    Fax: 617-742-3933

MICHIGAN

Michigan Housing Coalition
Kris Wisniewski/Therese Porn
P.O. Box 14038
Lansing, MI 48901
    Phone: 517-377-0509
    Handsnet: HN0265

Michigan Housing Coordinating Council
Ted S. Rozeboom
309 North Washington Square, Suite 203
P.O. Box 30249
Lansing, MI 48909
    Phone: 517-335-0923

MINNESOTA

Interagency Task Force on Homelessness
Minnesota Housing Finance Agency
James Solem
400 Sibley Street, Suite 300
St. Paul, MN 55101
    Phone: 612-296-7608
    Fax: 612-296-8139
    Handsnet: HN0731

Minnesota Coalition for the Homeless
Val Baertlein/Sue Watlov Phillips
668 Broadway Street, NE
Minneapolis, MN 55413
    Phone: 612-379-8920
    Handsnet: HN1104

Minnesota Housing Partnership
Chip Halbach
520 20th Avenue, S.
Minneapolis, MN 55454
    Phone: 612-339-5255

Minnesota Department of Jobs and Training
Patrick Leary
150 East Kellogg Boulevard, Suite 670
St. Paul, MN 55101
    Phone: 612-297-3409
    Fax: 612-296-5745

MISSISSIPPI

Governor's Office of Federal/State Programs
Community Services Branch
Larry Christian
421 West Pascagoula Street
Jackson, MS 39203
    Phone: 601-949-2041, ext. 4266

Mississippi Housing Coalition
Linda McMurtrey
P.O. Box 373
Jackson, MS 39205
    Phone: 601-545-4595
    Fax: 601-545-4608
    Handsnet: HN0337

Mississippi Task Force on Homelessness
Department of Finance and Administration
Divison of Budget and Policy
Royal Walker
455 N. Lamar Street
Jackson, MS 39202
    Phone: 601-359-6753
    Fax: 601-359-2405

MISSOURI

Division of General Services
Department of Social Services
Al Gage
P.O. Box 1643
Jefferson City, MO 65102
    Phone: 314-751-3870
    Fax: 314-751-1329

Low Income Housing Task Force
Missouri Association for Social Welfare
Peter DeSimone
515 East High Street
Jefferson City, MO 65101
    Phone: 314-634-2901

Missouri Coalition for the Homeless
Larry Rice
c/o New Life Evangelistic Center
P.O. Box 473
St. Louis, MO 63166
    Phone: 314-421-3020 or 314-896-9109

MONTANA

Intergovernmental Human Services Bureau
Family Services Division
Department of Social and Rehab Services
Jim Nolan
P.O. Box 4210
Helena, MT 59604
    Phone: 406-444-4540
    Fax: 406-444-1970

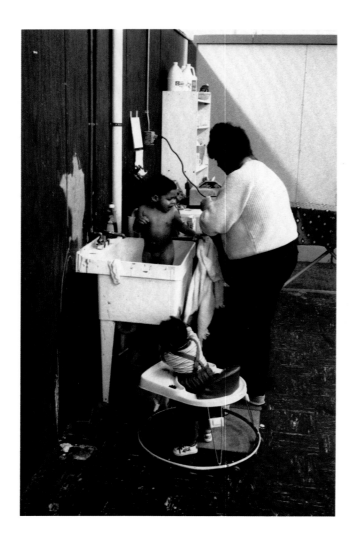

94

Montana Low Income Coalition
Marcia Schreder
P.O. Box 1029
Helena, MT 59624
    Phone: 406-449-8801

NEBRASKA

Governor's Policy Research Office
Gary L. Rex
State Capitol, Suite 1319
Lincoln, NE 68509
    Phone: 402-471-2414
    Fax: 402-471-2063

Nebraska Coalition for the Homeless
John Mata
3915 "N" Street
Omaha, NE 68107
    Phone: 402-559-7115

NEVADA

Nevada Homeless Coalition
Nancy Paolini
c/o Department of Social Work
University of Nevada/Reno, Mail Stop 90
Reno, NV 89557
    Phone: 702-784-6542

Nevada State Welfare Division
Linda A. Ryan/Anthoula Sullivan
2527 North Carson Street
Carson City, NV 89710
    Phone: 702-687-4715
    Fax: 702-687-5080

NEW HAMPSHIRE

New Hampshire Coalition for the Homeless
Henrietta Charest
P.O. Box 46
Manchester, NH 03105
    Phone: 603-623-4888

New Hampshire Commission on Homelessness
Msgr. John Quinn
c/o New Hampshire Catholic Charities
P.O. Box 686
Manchester, NH 03105
    Phone: 603-669-3030

Office of the Governor/State of New Hampshire
Nancy Baybutt
State Capitol
Concord, NH 03301
    Phone: 603-271-2121
    Fax: 603-271-2130

NEW JERSEY

Governor's Office of Management and Planning
Christina Klotz
State House, CN-001
Trenton, NJ 08625
    Phone: 609-777-1265
    Fax: 609-392-6193

New Jersey Department of Community Affairs, AHMS
Anthony Cancro
101 South Broad Street
CN 806
Trenton, NJ 08625-0806
    Phone: 609-292-9795
    Fax: 609-633-2132

Right to Housing Coalition of New Jersey
Peggy Earisman
217 Howe Avenue
Passaic, NJ 07055
    Phone: 201-932-6812 (Tricia Fagan)
    Handsnet: HN0161

NEW MEXICO

Human Services Department
Community Assistance Section/Income Support Divison
Dorian Dodson
P.O. Box 2348
Santa Fe, NM 87504
    Phone: 505-827-7264
    Fax: 505-827-8480

New Mexico Housing Coalition
Michael A. Varela
P.O. Box "CC"
Santa Fe, NM 87502
    Phone: 505-988-2859

NEW YORK

Housing Now: New York City/State
Larry Wood
c/o Cathedral of St. John the Divine
1047 Amsterdam Avenue
New York City, NY 10025
    Phone: 212-316-7544

New York State Coalition for the Homeless
Fred Griesbach
90 State Street, Suite 1505
Albany, NY 12207
    Phone: 518-436-5612
    Fax: 518-436-5615
    Handsnet: HN0158

New York State Rural Housing Coalition
Tim Palmer
350 Northern Boulevard, Suite 101-102
Albany, NY 12210
    Phone: 518-434-1314

Office of Shelter and Supportive Housing Programs
Department of Social Services
Peter R. Brest
40 North Pearl Street, Floor 10-A
Albany, NY 12243
    Phone: 518-474-9059 or 212-804-1295
    Fax: 518-474-9004

NORTH CAROLINA

Division of Community Assistance
Bob Chandler/Deborah G. McCrae
1307 Glenwood Avenue, Suite 250
Raleigh, NC 27605
    Phone: 919-733-2850
    Fax: 919-733-5262
    Handsnet: HN0952

North Carolina Low Income Housing Coalition
Linda Shaw
P.O. Box 27863
Raleigh, NC 27611
    Phone: 919-833-6201
    Handsnet: HN0152

NORTH DAKOTA

North Dakota Coalition for Homeless People
Barbara Stanton
c/o YWCA
1616 12th Avenue, North
Fargo, ND 58102
    Phone: 701-232-2547

Office of Intergovernmental Assistance
Shirley Dykshoorn
State Capitol Building, 14th floor
Bismarck, ND 58505
    Phone: 701-224-2094
    Fax: 701-224-3000

OHIO

Office of the Governor/Human Services
Executive Assistant
77 South High Street, 30th floor
Columbus, OH 43266
    Phone: 614-466-7781
    Fax: 614-466-9354

Ohio Coalition for the Homeless
Bill Faith
1066 North High Street
Columbus, OH 43201
    Phone: 614-291-1984
    Fax: 614-291-2009
    Handsnet: HN0159

Ohio Department of Development/Community Development
Roberta ("Bobbie") Garber
P.O. Box 1001
Columbus, OH 43266
    Phone: 614-466-5863
    Fax: 614-466-4708

Ohio Department of Mental Health
Interagency Homeless Cluster
Attn: Assistant Director
30 East Broad Street
Columbus, OH 43215
   Phone: 614-466-7460

Ohio Housing Coalition
Julie A. Keil
1066 North High Street
Columbus, OH 43201
   Phone: 614-299-0544
   Handsnet: HN0351

Ohio Rural Housing Coalition
Roger McCauley
P.O. Box 787
Athens, OH 45701
   Phone: 614-594-8499
   Fax: 614-592-5994

OKLAHOMA

Governor's Task Force on Homelessness
Robert Fulton
Office of the Governor
State Capitol, Suite 210
Oklahoma City, OK 73105
   Phone: 405-523-4254

Oklahoma Housing Finance Agency/Homeless Programs
Shirley Williams
P.O. Box 26720
Oklahoma City, OK 73126
   Phone: 405-848-1144
   Fax: 405-842-2537

OREGON

Oregon Housing Now Coalition
Mickey Clay/José Mata
c/o Lutheran Office on Public Policy
2710 NE 14th Avenue
Portland, OR 97212
    Phone: 503-288-0317

Oregon Rural Housing Coalition
Darlee Rex
525 Glen Creek Road, NW, Suite 210
Salem, OR 97304
    Phone: 503-585-6193

Oregon Shelter Network
Robert B. More
370 South Second Street
Coos Bay, OR 97420
    Phone: 503-269-0443

State Community Services
Victor Vasquez/Alan Kramer
1158 Chemeketa Street, NE
Salem, OR 97310
    Phone: 503-378-4729
    Fax: 503-378-8467

PENNSYLVANIA

Coalition on Homelessness in Pennsylvania
Phyllis Ryan
802 North Broad Street
Philadelphia, PA 19130
    Phone: 215-232-2300

Governor's Policy Office
Annette Mayer
Finance Building, Suite 506
Harrisburg, PA 17120
    Phone: 717-787-1954
    Fax: 717-787-8614

Pennsylvania Low Income Housing Coalition
Mary Ann Holloway
4 South Easton Road
Glenside, PA 19038
    Phone: 215-576-7044

PUERTO RICO

Coalition for the Rights of the Homeless
Gloria Ruiz de Marti
G.P.O. 3603
San Juan, PR 00936
    Phone: 809-722-1910 or 809-724-4051

Office of Federal Affairs/Office of the Governor
Fernando Lloveras-San Miguel, Esq.
La Fortaleza
P.O. Box 82
San Juan, PR 00901
    Phone: 809-721-7000
    Fax: 809-721-5072

RHODE ISLAND

Division of Economic and Social Services
Department of Human Services
Thomas A. McDonough
600 New London Avenue
Cranston, RI 02920
    Phone: 401-464-2371
    Fax: 401-464-1876

Rhode Island Coalition for the Homeless
David McCreadie, Jr.
P.O. Box 23505
Providence, RI 02903
   Phone: 401-421-6458

Rhode Island Right to Housing Coalition
Jim Tull
c/o Amos House
P.O. Box 2873
Providence, RI 02907
   Phone: 401-272-0220

SOUTH CAROLINA

Economic Opportunity Division
William E. Gunn
1205 Pendleton Street, Suite 357
Columbia, SC 29201
   Phone: 803-734-0662
   Fax: 803-734-0356

South Carolina Coalition for the Homeless
Marie Toner
c/o South Carolina Department of Social Services
P.O. Box 1520
Columbia, SC 29202
   Phone: 803-734-6183
   Fax: 803-734-5597
   Handsnet: 1-800-868-3677

South Carolina Low Income Housing Coalition
Marvin Lare
P.O. Box 1520
Columbia, SC 29202
   Phone: 803-734-6122
   Fax: 803-734-5597
   Handsnet: 1-800-868-3677

South Carolina Citizens for Housing
Linda Ketner
1 North Adjer's Wharf
Charleston, SC 29401
   Phone: 803-723-9966

SOUTH DAKOTA

Office of the Governor
Ruth Hultgren Henneman
State Capitol Building
Pierre, SD 57501
   Phone: 605-773-3212
   Fax: 605-773-4711

TENNESSEE

Tennessee Coalition for the Homeless
Ed J. Wallin
c/o Veterans Center
1 North Third Street
Memphis, TN 38103
   Phone: 901-544-3506

Tennessee Department of Human Services
Steven Meinbresse
Citizens Plaza
Nashville, TN 37248
   Phone: 615-741-3335
   Fax: 615-741-4165

TEXAS

Texas Alliance for Human Needs
Jude Filler
2520 Longview, Suite 311
Austin, TX 78705
    Phone: 512-474-5019

Texas Department of Community Affairs
General Willie L. Scott/Eddie Fariss
P.O. Box 13166
Austin, TX 78711
    Phone: 512-834-6022

Texas Homeless Network
Kent C. Miller
c/o Benedictine Health Service
400 East Anderson Lane, Suite 306
Austin, TX 78752
    Phone: 512-339-9724

UTAH

State Homeless Coordinating Committee
Department of Community and Economic Development
Kerry Bate
324 South State Street, 3rd floor
Salt Lake City, UT 84111
    Phone: 801-538-8723
    Fax: 801-538-8888

Utah Housing Coalition
Mark Smith
c/o Independent Living Center
764 South 200th West
Salt Lake City, UT 84101
    Phone: 801-359-2444

VERMONT

Department of Housing and Community Affairs
Nancy Eldridge
Pavilion Building
Montpelier, VT 05602
    Phone: 802-828-3217
    Fax: 802-828-3339

Rural Vermont
Anthony Pollina
15 Barre Street
Montpelier, VT 05602
    Phone: 802-223-7222

Vermont Affordable Housing Coalition
Kirby A. Dunn
P.O. Box 1603
Burlington, VT 05402
    Phone: 802-863-6248

Vermont Coalition for the Homeless/Vermont Housing
Now/COTS
Lucille Bonvouloir
P.O. Box 1616
Burlington, VT 05402
    Phone: 802-864-7402

VIRGINIA

Rural Virginia, Inc.
Rich Cagan
P.O. Box 105
Richmond, VA 23201
    Phone: 804-524-5853

Southwest Virginia Housing Coalition
Appalachian Office of Peace and Justice
Anthony Flaccavento
P.O. Box 660
St. Paul, VA 24283
  Phone: 703-762-5050

Virginia Coalition for the Homeless
Sue M. Capers
7825 Cherokee Road
Richmond, VA 23225
  Phone: 804-320-4577

Virginia Housing Coalition
John McCrimmon
c/o Williamsburg/James
City/County Community Action Agency
P.O. Box H-K
Williamsburg, VA 23187
  Phone: 804-229-9332

Virginia Department of Housing and Community Development
Robert J. Adams/Irene Clouse
205 North 4th Street
Richmond, VA 23219
  Phone: 804-786-5395
  Fax: 804-225-3822

VIRGIN ISLANDS

Advocates for the Homeless
Thyra Budsan/Chris Finch
c/o United Way
P.O. Box 6168
St. Thomas, VI 00804
  Phone: 809-774-3185

Department of Planning and Natural Resources
Division of Capital and Development Planning
Jasmine Gunthorpe
Nisky Center, Suite 231
Charlotte Amalie
St. Thomas, VI 00802
  Phone: 809-774-3320

WASHINGTON

Emergency Housing Services
Department of Community Development
Corine Foster
9th and Columbia Building, MS/GH-51
Olympia, WA 98504
  Phone: 206-586-1363
  Fax: 206-586-5880

Housing Trust Fund Coalition
Sharon Lee
c/o Fremont Public Association
P.O. Box 31151
Seattle, WA 98103
  Phone: 206-548-8374
  Fax: 206-548-8359
  Handsnet: HN0304

Washington Coalition for Rural Housing
Kurt Creager
19021 90th Place, Northeast
Bothell, WA 98011
  Phone: 206-296-8644

Washington Low Income Housing Coalition
Ken Katahira
c/o Inter *IM
409 Maynard, South
Seattle, WA 98104
  Phone: 206-624-1802

Washington State Coalition for the Homeless
Maureen Howard/Margaret Maxwell
P.O. Box 955
Tacoma, WA 98401
    Phone: 206-572-4237 or 206-383-1585
    Fax: 206-383-0776

WEST VIRGINIA

Office of Economic Opportunity
Community Development Division
Isiah C. Lineberry
1204 Kanawha Boulevard, East
Charleston, WV 25301
    Phone: 304-348-8860

Office of Economic Opportunity
Community Development Division
Governor's Office of Community and Industrial Development
Joseph L. Barker
1204 Kanawha Boulevard, East
Charleston, WV 25301
    Phone: 304-348-4010

West Virginia Coalition for the Homeless
Chuck Hamsher
1205 Quarrier Street, 1st Floor
Charleston, WV 25301
    Phone: 304-344-3970
    Handsnet: HN0167

WISCONSIN

Department of Health and Social Services
Patricia Goodrich
1 West Wilson Street
P.O. Box 7850
Madison, WI 53707
    Phone: 608-266-3681
    Fax: 608-266-7882

Foundation for Rural Housing, Inc.
Char Thompson
4506 Regent Street
Madison, WI 53705
    Phone: 608-238-3448

Governor's Interagency Coordinating Committee
Division of Economic Support/DHSS
Judith Wilcox (Homeless Shelter Coordinator)
P.O. Box 7935
Madison, WI 53707
    Phone: 608-266-9388
    Fax: 608-267-3240

WYOMING

Division of Community Programs
Department of Health and Social Services
Gary E. Maier
2300 Capitol Avenue
Cheyenne, WY 82002
    Phone: 307-777-6779
    Fax: 307-777-6289

Wyoming Against Homelessness
Virginia D. Sellner
c/o COMEA Shelter
P.O. Box 15566
Cheyenne, WY 82003
    Phone: 307-632-3174

Homeless activist Mitch Snyder being arrested.

PHOTOGRAPHS

107